Poems for Peace

First published in 2015

Cover illustration: by NoBoDy

Cover design by NoBoDy

Printed by Biddles Books, King's Lynn, Norfolk PE32 1SF

For my Uncle, Richard 'Clicker' Kleiser,

who always wanted Peace

'Emancipate yourselves from mental slavery, none but ourselves can free our minds.'

- Bob Marley

Poems for Peace

Editor

Poppy Kleiser

Fenland Poet Laureate 2014

Contents

Foreword

Benjamin Zephaniah

War, what is it good for? Absolutely nothing. So said that often quoted song lyric from 1969, and it is often quoted sarcastically by those who believe it makes a nice pop song, but it's too simplistic. The truth is that sometimes the truth is simple. War is bad. Simple, but true. War has achieved very little in real terms, and almost any gains that the defenders of wars can point to are very short lived. The truth is, there is no way to peace, peace is the way, but in a world where politicians (both male and female) have a macho, 'might is right' approach to politics, peace will always be seen as just an absence of war, or a space in-between wars. So as they send young women and men to war they will tell you that they are fighting for peace, or that this war is the war to end wars.

Now even organisations like the Norwegian Nobel Committee can give peace prizes to people who have spent their lives fighting, and we are told that they deserve the prize because they have stopped fighting. Yet people who genuinely dedicate their lives to working for peace are called radicals, alternatives, soft or dreamers. The harsh reality is that if for some unimaginable reason peace broke out tomorrow the streets would not be filled with people celebrating, but there would be people from the arms trade complaining about the loss of their jobs and the 'death' of a great

British industry.

Films might glorify war, electronics games might trivialise war, but the role of the poet is to think deeply about war, by discarding the notion of winners and losers and bringing some emotional intelligence to the subject. The poets in this collection have imaginatively scanned theatres of war with compassionate and caring eyes, so when one of our poets tell us that 'Boys – Become no more than matchsticks – Sent home in boxes', it doesn't take much to understand that this can apply to anyone sent to war, from any side of any man made divide.

Warmongers will sit comfortably in their offices, or appear on your televisions sets and tell you that their war is a just war, and that the army builds you up and makes you brave, but the reality for most people, (and most people know this), is as one of our poets said of her father 'They broke you down, took away the bravery'. She goes on to say 'My father made me a solider - But I'll fight these wars with words'. And this is a major theme in this collection. Some of the poets are angry, some are thoughtful, some are searching, some are intellectual, but they are all questioning and learning the lessons of war, their tools are their 'selves' and their words. They are learning from the lessons of the past, they are exploring the universal truths, and not constructing strategic answers.

No war will end wars. You can bomb the world into pieces, but you can't bomb it into peace. The monsters you create today will return to destroy you tomorrow. Politicians might struggle with these simple concepts, but the poet must keep reminding them of these home truths. They are telling us to commemorate wars with displays of pomp and ceremony, they build monuments and tell us to bow before them, they stand in awe in the presence of the killing machines that they themselves have created, but they refuse to learn the lessons of war, moreover they even refuse to learn from their own mistakes, and their own bloody history. If they will not learn, if they will not listen to mothers crying for their dead children, if they will not hear those who take to the streets to say that there is another way, then we who love poetry, we who appreciate art regardless of where it comes from, can also appreciate the oneness of this diverse collection of poets. We can connect with the creativity of the voices in these poet's heads, and we can see that the poets gathered here between these pages, have in their own ways, seen the ugliness of war, and rejected the glorification of this brutality. Poets are beautiful, poetry is a beautiful thing.

Benjamin Zephaniah

Alison Brackenbury

'In a Lincolnshire village, in the late 1950s, on Saturday afternoons, I would listen raptly to my grandfather's stories of the First World War. He could still sing a spirited version of 'Mademoiselle from Armentières'. Unfortunately, he was not regarded by the family as a very reliable narrator! But I still believe some of his stories, including those about an animal rarely mentioned in summaries of the Great War.

I grew up in the Lincolnshire countryside, and am descended from long lines of domestic servants, gamekeepers and prizewinning shepherds. I migrated down the limestone to Gloucestershire, where I now live. Along the way, I was a student at Oxford, a librarian in a technical college, a metal finisher in my husband's family business, a parent, and owner of far too many cats and unaffordable ponies.

I have also written nine collections of poems, some of which have been broadcast on national radio. The diverse influences on my work include my industrial job and my stubborn passion for folk songs. I am now retired, so find myself suddenly whizzing around doing numerous readings, recording for Radio 4, etc. My poems can now be heard at the Poetry Archive: www.poetryarchive.org

My latest collection is *Then* (Carcanet, 2013). Gillian Clarke, the National Poet of Wales, commented: ‘Alison Brackenbury loves, lives, hymns and rhymes the natural world and its people like no other poet.’ The poem in this anthology, ‘Told’, will appear in my next collection, due very early in 2016 from Carcanet.’
www.alisonbrackenbury.co.uk

Told

Ask everything you want to!
You cannot stay long.
No one, now, will ever hear
your father's father's songs.

I heard both songs and stories
from my mother's father's war.
But, in forty years,
he grew a joyful liar.

He had seen every truce,
the football in the mud,
stood, he said, a batman, ironing,
to the great guns' thud.

No one else spoke of the mules,
led where no rail could run,
of axles, bubbling under mud
where useless wheels spun.

So every story ended
as his lame wife laid for three,

‘Then the mule kicked the Major –
so we laughed and drank our tea.’
Then the mule kicked the Major.
So we laughed, and drank our tea.

Alison Brackenbury

William Alderson

William Alderson has been writing poetry since he was nine. He is a member of Cambridge Pub Poets, Downham Market Poets and Fen Speak. Despite sending out his poems only sporadically, he has been published in 14 magazines, including Envoi, Orbis, Ore, Haiku Quarterly, Pennine Platform and Staple. Two of his poems appeared in Cloudburst 2, a collection of poems by the Cambridge Pub Poets published in 2013.

He worked for 25 years in BBC Television News, mainly as a video editor. He trained on film and was the first person to edit an 'on-the-day' story for the BBC news on computer. He still publishes videos on YouTube. Many of his poems reflect his experience of the news and how it is reported.

'This poem was written in 2003 not long after the start of the war on Iraq. I was a founder of King's Lynn StoptheWar which argued against the war for reasons which have proved only too correct. At that time the overwhelming majority of people in Britain were opposed to the war, and two million people had joined the largest ever protest march in history. As a result, those who supported the war could not use their usual tactic of drowning out opposition. I know that the BBC did try, because I was working in BBC Television News and had been for many years. Instead the supporters of the war encouraged silence on the subject – in the interests of promoting harmony! I was particularly shocked to find this occurring in schools and universities and among some Quakers, who are justifiably famous for their opposition to war. In these circumstances, silence was clearly not neutral but an endorsement of the slaughter of civilian men, women and children and a grave for the truth.'

Truth

You have chosen silence as a place
Where somehow the truth can be found more easily,
Where emotions cannot cloud the stillness of judgement.
You trust the peace of the ivory tower or the ivory smile.

As if ... !

As if the thunder never happened
Among the white suspension of the clouds,
The houses of learning or the gardens of peace.

It is not just the elephants who die
To give you your delicate cage, your statues,
Your millennia of silence and nuance.

In Basra, Baghdad, Nasiriyah, Najaf ...
The water stations fall silent
The generators fall silent
The radios fall silent
The telephones fall silent
The voices fall silent
The children fall silent
And the mothers cry

With the birth pangs of a grief
Shared for the first time by a whole world,
And we know that we must cry out together
So loudly that even in the deadly silence of Iraq
They will know that life is born again
To suckle and grow
And challenge the deaf ears with the question "Why?"

William Alderson

Paul Quant

'As a little boy, standing in the garden of my home beside the busy A17 road at Long Sutton, I had watched convoys of military vehicles pass by, witnessed droning flights of military aircraft overhead and met several confused itinerant ex-military personnel who had come to our door seeking for money, food or shelter. This was in 1949 and the Second World War was only just in the past.

Although I was too young to be aware of the upheavals that accompanied the war, nevertheless I sensed the subversive grip it had had on the community. I imagine all wars to be like that and I have tried to express this idea in my poem.'

Unseen Depths

Slow running river pads the land along,
mildly dragging down towards the North Sea's door,
though that comes later, ending of the song.
Time slows the meanwhile, and the mind's deep store
climbs up the grass bank's slippery nettled side
to see the water's mirroring let slowly by
slight clouds, a dream of sometime high up ride
above this map into the silent sky.
Although contrasting with the fen drain's view,
behind him, fields grow green with silky winter wheat,
so dense and unpretentious, old yet new,
potato rows and spikes of seedling beet.

Stands on the flat bank for some minutes more,
as into sight there floats a motor boat that growls
its diesel engine, heading for that door
where waves are skinned and crusty danger prowls.
A hand is waved, returned, suggestions of
a hint to climb aboard to see what lies ahead.
But not for high bank watcher; his the love
that turned, slipped down again then onwards led
through all those simple, ordinary lanes
he's always known and never wants to leave behind.

Deny the challenge of these fenland plains
he will not do; he has a close-cropped mind.
A sense of duty? King and country need
his help and who is he to speak against the tide
that almost overwhelms him, throw his creed
upon that heap of bodies opened wide
by mortar fire, machine gun, cannonade.
That boat ties up and other locals climb aboard
with laughing faces. Will his faith now fade?
No, in the water's depths he hurls his sword.

Paul Quant

Peter Irving

Peter Irving was Peterborough's Poet Laureate for 2014 and is well known for his witty style and rambunctious performances.
Despite having a degree in Ecology, Peter remains an optimist and is committed to the promotion of the Spoken Arts, Peterborough and its citizens.
'Hits you like a drunken sumo wrestler!' University Press

'Sadly the poem is based on real events in Peterborough and the casualty figures are from the Museum archives/records: I think the numbers speak for themselves.'

Peterborough Pals

Me and 166 footballing chums
took Kitchener's shilling
to hammer the Huns.
Engineers and apprentices
swopped overalls for khaki,
joined up in our football teams
Whitsted's, Werner's and Perkins,
just playing in a different league
a million volunteers
in that season's kick-off:
September 1914.

Kicking a ball as we advance
weaving between craters and wire
all dreaming of scoring *that* goal
and winning *this* war.
British lions, a Pal's Battalion,
out in the mud and gas
between Fletton football ground
and that final whistle in *No Man's Land*.

Fixed in a frame
my team mates remain,
uniform faded, but eyes unchanged,
all singing *'Tipperary'*
as we joined the troop-train.
166 left our factory gates,
but I returned with 15 of my mates,
just enough to make one team
amidst the unseen barbed wire
of empty pitches in 1918.

Peter Irving

Mike Alderson

Mike has had 40 poems published before producing the book *Surviving the Institutions*. It is a combination of the poems written over the years he spent working with people with learning disabilities and photos taken with his sister (the photo artist Jane Alderson), of the two hospitals where these people lived.

Since moving to Peterborough and Deeping, Mike has performed regularly with *Poetry United*, *Pint of Poetry* at Peterborough and *Pint of Poetry* at Stamford. He has performed at the Family Tent at the Cambridge Folk Festival on occasions. He did a 3 venue tour in Bristol promoting his book. With Pint of Poetry he has appeared at the Edinburgh Fringe 2012 and 2013.

Mike set up Bristol's first regular poetry in performance venue, *Second Tuesday*, in January 1987. It is still going after various mutations as *Poetry Can*. Mike ran performance groups: *Rats for Love* then *Dead Rats on Leave* in Bristol through 1987 to 1991. Mike and/or the *Rats* performed at Art Centres, Poetry groups, pubs, festivals and other venues in Bristol, Bath, Gloucester and Somerset. He also came fourth in the Ware Open Competition (2013).

Mike has run workshops, e.g. for the John Clare Festival at Peterborough Museum and in schools.

See him perform at the Edinburgh Fringe at:

Pint of Poetry Ed Fringe 2012 Show 1, Part 4 of 7 Mike Alderson - YouTube

Gulf 1991

Rain splashes a moment, out of place,
pale sky sucking out sweat.
Wipers smear dirt, censor vision.
Through the windscreen
I look for outlines.

In silences, calculations of chance
digging each side of a border,
air infesting lungs,
spreading narrow cemeteries
through sand.

Heat simmers. Between orders:
vomit of fear,
politics of firepower, siege.
Censors cloud old alliances,
recycle histories.

Parked on the kerb, I wind
down windows to clear the air,

check the petrol gauge,

and wonder when the bodies

will come home.

Mike Alderson

Helen Pletts

This poem highlights some of the many violently extreme ways in which the CIA attempted to assassinate Fidel Castro and overthrow his political allies.

'I wrote the poem for my father, Mike Bannister, after we had read and marvelled at the incredibly large amount of planned or actual attempts on Castro's life - 638 in all!'

Don't try to change the course of Cuban History

By sending exploding cigars, an agent
with a pen-syringe, approaching underworld figures
to carry out a killing, placing high explosives
under the speaker's podium, recruiting

an old classmate to shoot someone dead
in the street in broad daylight, enlisting
a former lover as an assassin
armed with poison pills, buying Caribbean

molluscs with a view to planting explosives
in the largest shell, preparing
a skin disease infected diving suit,
making bacterial poisons

to be placed in a handkerchief or
in a cup of tea or coffee, rigging up
a radio station with noxious gas, using snipers,
blowing up an airliner.

Helen Pletts

Keely Mills

Keely has been writing poetry for over 15 years and her personal career highlights include being the Peterborough Poet Laureate for 2009 and producing a successful poetry night in Peterborough for over 4 years with co-producer and poet Mark Grist. Keely has also performed right across the UK at festivals, workshops, W.I. luncheons and in theatre spaces.

Keely has either worked or performed with Attila the Stockbroker, Kate Tempest, Benjamin Zephaniah, John Cooper Clarke, Germaine Greer, Scroobius Pip and David Morley. Her poetry commissions have included writing for Peterborough City Council planning reports, Heritage Lottery Funded projects and for particular issues such as land rights, mental health awareness, women's rights and Gypsy and Traveller rights.

Keely is currently working on her first Arts Council funded show which is called 'You Can't Be Surprised By a Selfie' and she hopes this will tour in 2015. Find out more about her at: http://keelymills.wordpress.com/

'My poem *Sean-na-chie-* , about the Highland Clearances, is a result of pure anger towards an event or series of events that not only made a few even richer, but changed the landscape of an entire country, decimating whole communities in a cruel and brutal way.

All the different deeds described in the poem *did* happen and it really shocked me how this part of our history is not talked about. What I found really compelling was the idea that this intrusive and ridiculous statue (that still exists as a monument to one of the clearances' worst perpetrators) should not be torn down but actually neglected and left to rot. Remembered but not maintained or worshipped. This gave me the idea that Scotland might be on to something.'

Sean-na-chie-

*A folk historian amongst the Highlanders of Scotland whose calling was to witness and to keep the memory of the experiences of their community alive.

I

The bleeding clotted words from scarred wounds, become stories
that never really heal, often pricked by the memories of cleansing
fires and these lesions are cut deep as the mount of Canada Hill.
Where Clansmen climbed with their tartan stripped from waist, land
and family, to spy the ships that leave for new endeavours. Eyes of
grief capture their brothers' faces in stormy clouds before their last
blinkered glimpse of them forever.
Improvements came in the year of the sheep. Sweeping away
bristling highland peaks as the ling heather is harvested in August,
nature left strange and barren. Waves of pinkish lilac turn into the
crushed heads of the women of Strathcarron.
Their punctured stern beauty, beaten by the landlord's craven militia
who charged the unarmed daughters of Ross-shire. Struck them with
all their force, mangling limbs and weltering gore lying them down
in fields of savage mire.

II

The act of union that was burned in the dead of Cullodden gave way to George's butcher to sever tribes through their stomachs being emptied and their tongues being levered. A Duke, devoid of the spirit of kindness triggered the murdering, raping of all that came across his suspicious heart, now maimed and now tethered. Proscription quietened all song with the Gaelic 'dia duit' that hoped some God would be with them, no more would the kinsfolk meet to gather tales and rebellion. Ere the shapes of men were culled into chattels for the harsh watery graves of kelp work or bound to be new slaves of the Caribbean.

Displaced crofters held their possessions in the rain, no abode awaiting their weary bodies when their forty mile trek was done. Yet their legs carried many a soul when the sea of flames flooded the blazing houses that scalded for six days till there was none. Their ashes could not dry the cries of dashed hopes that soon crashed on the rocks of Strath point.

The clearance of Barra was an artful plan by cunning Cluny a colonel who called his tenants to a meeting that would never be minuted. With threats of blazing destruction the village of 1,500 breaths, were bound to go to the assembly hall like cattle unaware of the sorrow ahead.

III

These people were seized, with handcuffs and truncheons that smashed all the power from them. Dragged onto the ship bound for lands that lived over the horizon, some broke free into the sombre ocean, swimming for Scotland. Yet only finding the police's felling hand and their bankrupt wanderings of Glasgow's streets.

No one was better than the Duke of Sutherland at pulling the plough up in the rafters and replacing them with the big white sheep in a vile landslide. Their teeth lay many a man upon a shelf and the jaws of Stafford bit a broad mark into the countryside. Chewing the limbs of his thousand dwellers in a greed for the profit of coin over mortals, the pains of revenue
he would neither starve nor deny.

With a winter came a death that birthed plans that would rub scorn into foundations of stone that would burrow into the heathland. A monument to honour the first marquis of eviction, slow deaths and dishonours, was built upon a terrifying demand. Those who he had turfed from grass to beach in life were threatened with a spectre of consequence, if they did not raise a shilling to pay for a statue that still sits upon Ben Braggie in sick prominence.

A 100 feet effigy that looks over the skyline of Golspie, still stands
as a reminder that some ranks will take the benefits of money over
the cares of man. Angers tear into the wind and there is still a hand
that would slash its features till gloating eyes became mineral again.
Sean-na-chie's would pray that a hundred years from now this
would be a pedestal of crumbling decay, never forgotten but ravaged
by the nature he tried in life to tame.

Keely Mills

Poppy Kleiser

Poppy Kleiser was Fenland Poet Laureate for 2014. Influenced by folk song and the radicalism of 18th century Romantic literature, she attempts through both written and spoken word to explore the secrets of the strange and haunting place she lives.

She has performed widely; from festivals to exhibitions and shows about land rights history. Much of her work is written with nature as a guiding force.

Poppy is passionate about pacifism as a proactive stance; she believes that in order to make peace we cannot be passive. She realises there are a lot of P's in that sentence.

Digging was inspired by a trip to the Flanders Fields in Belgium.

Digging

An unknown soldier from an absent land
Would wash away the world with thoughts of home
Dug out the ditches so much like his own
And ripped the air with screams of phantom seas.
At home they dug for life, he thought –
Despite the slitting of the wicker catch, although
They cut the legs from crouching snigglers, who
Moon-mad leapt from pool to vapoured ditch.
They slink like eels around the sculpted veins, like
Let us onto land, let us be the start of life again, those sparkling cells
Green and laughing, let us see the rivers fresh from blood and for this
Prehistoric race let us breathe the air again.

He once had known a girl at home, who lived upon the ten mile bank
Who had the sting of sea salt on her skin, who
Called the echoed song of ghostly birds
And as the soldier felt the fire and died, upon the fen he heard the mermaid sing.

Poppy Kleiser

Leanne Moden

Over three hundred British and Commonwealth soldiers were shot for desertion and cowardice during the First World War. It’s a shocking figure. Many of those executed were no older than twenty. They had signed up to fight for what they believed to be a noble cause, only to be traumatised and terrified by the horrors of war.

But what circumstances could cause a man to leave his post despite knowing that to do so would mean certain death? Were these people cowards, traitors, or victims? Did any of them really deserve to die?

Although it's important not to view the past through the prism of our modern values, it's hard not to feel some sympathy for these young men, and these feelings are expressed in the poem, *Witness*.
In the context of modern conflict, the poem also reflects the execution of hostages in wars across the globe, and the importance of continuing to speak out against violence and injustice.

Leanne Moden is a performance poet from Cambridgeshire. She was Fenland Poet Laureate in 2013, and Poet in Residence at the *Museum of Beyond* in 2014. She also researched and wrote a non-fiction book – published by University of Hertfordshire Press – and her poetry has appeared in several anthologies and literary magazines.

Leanne has performed at festivals and events across the UK including Bestival, the Aldeburgh Poetry Festival, Folk East and the Beverley Folk Festival. In summer 2014, Leanne reached the quarter finals of the Hammer and Tongue UK Slam Championships, and performing at the Royal Albert Hall has been a career highlight. Leanne is also a founding member of the *28 Sonnets Later* writers' collective, and co-host of the *Fen Speak* poetry open mic nights.

Witness

I have tasted dust and blood
And felt the shrapnel's sting.
I have moved among the dead
And witnessed everything.

I have dodged the rounds and shells
And heard the bullets sing.
I have moved among the dead
And witnessed everything.

I have felt the fear and shame
Creep beneath my skin.
I have moved among the dead
And witnessed everything.

Some will call it cowardice,
Betraying kith and kin,
But I have moved among the dead
And witnessed everything.

Mortar-worn, I ran from hell
And that's my only sin.
I have moved among the dead
And witnessed everything.

So fasten feathers to my coat –
I'll scarcely feel the pin.
For I have moved among the dead,
And witnessed everything.

And I will raise my blindfold
When the firing squad begins,
So when they shoot between my eyes
I'll witness everything.

And when they write our history,
Please pencil my name in.
Honour me among the dead,
And witness everything.

Leanne Moden

Patrick Widdess

Patrick Widdess was born in Cambridge and has also lived in Greece, China, Japan and Poland. He was involved in the poetry and spoken word scene for many years in Cambridge as a performer at CB1 Poetry, Hammer and Tongue and Allographic, and as presenter of the radio show Headstand on Cambridge 105.
In 2014 he was a finalist in the Hammer and Tongue national slam final. His contribution to national WWI Centenary project Letter to the Unknown Soldier is due to appear in an anthology published by Harper Collins this winter.

He currently lives in Newport, South Wales.

Hands was inspired by the experiences of Shamsha, a 12-year-old girl caught in the conflict in Somalia.

Hands

Her scars are the words her hands can't write,
Mangled stumps on a body not yet full grown.

She was searching for her father.
There had been an attack.
Her mother had vanished four months ago
And brother too, lost in the city's torn sinews
Where her father may still be alive.

In the aftermath an explosion
Shook the neighbourhood and ripped her arms apart.

She would like them to see her,
Those who wave from the front pages of the paper.
Those who sign contracts and treaties,
Who lay wreaths and salute their troops.

Those whose hands move hands around the world
But didn't lift a finger the night she ended up in this hospital
Where her father may never find her.

Now other hands feed and tend her
But cannot repair the broken skin and shattered bones,
The flesh and blood too widely scattered to restore.

Patrick Widdess

James Knox Whittet

'I came across a copy of John Buxton's book on the Redstart - a small bird with a bright red tail - in my local library and was so impressed by it that I wanted to discover more about the author.

I read that he was a poet who had been posted to Norway as an Intelligence Officer and was captured by the Germans during the Second World War. He was taken to Laufen Castle, in Bavaria, which had been transformed into a prisoner of war camp.

He was a keen ornithologist and his years in prison were made endurable by his minute observation of the Redstart. One normally thinks of a free human being observing the antics of a bird in a cage but, in this case, we have a caged human observing a bird in its freedom. This brought home to me the absurdity of war and that we can learn, like John Buxton, from the mysterious laws of the natural world which surround us.'

Birds Viewed from a Cage

Day after day, I watch their
orange tails quiver in the cherry
trees, inhabiting a world not
of our corrupt, human making.

They find freedom following
laws they do not pause to question:
it is enough to fly, to eat, to feel
the sun's warmth on their feathers.

They are within our sight but beyond
our reach: they transcend our
suffering as rainbows arch over
the scarred fields of battle where later

the open eyes of the dead mirror
slow onsets of dusk like stagnant
pools. Myself and my fellow prisoners
grow thin and weaken; we long for

letters of home; vivid dreams assail
us each night as we shiver with fever
beneath coarse blankets stained with spit
blood; I feel her ghostly lips brush mine.

But dawn comes like a gash and then I
hear birdsong sound like the notes of that
piano I played as a child with the
metronome of raindrops on the attic roof.
I look out at the black faces and wings
of males who tiptoe across alien land,
more at ease in currents of air which
blows as if from some far off country.

I merge myself into their world and
away from my world of boredom
and pain. I become part of what I
observe: the boundaries which separate

us dissolve. Some nights, those bars
which cage me in fall away and I fly
like a bird from an opened cage
and feel the wash of air against my

orange plumage as I migrate across
oceans, hearing the wind and the
steady beat, beat of my wings:
my flight guided by invisible hands.

James Knox Whittet

Russell J Turner

Russell J Turner is a poet, actor and broadcaster based in Norwich. He is the founder and host of headCRASH productions, presenting spoken word nights since 2008. He is also the co-founder and co-host of Norwich Birdcage Slam.

He has performed featured slots at gigs and festivals across the country, been published in a number of print and online journals, and is a member of the 28 Sonnets Later collective: http://28SonnetsLater.blogspot.com

Between 2011 and 2013 he worked with Apples & Snakes and Writers' Centre Norwich on 'Shake the Dust' and 'Slam in a Box', two projects delivering youth slam workshops and competitions nationally, as well as developing a stand-alone youth slam model for schools and other organisations in the Eastern region.

Russell is currently developing his first live literature show, The Vodka Diaries, about the ups and downs of living with a bottle as your best friend.

"I have always been struck by the images of young men, workmates and friends, joining up en masse in solidarity with each other and their country, looking forward to the great adventure which would lead to so many of them crippled and dying. This is a story which has been told many times of course. But I have also always thought about the wives and sweethearts, mothers and sisters who were left behind. And this is a story which does not get told enough."

The Whistling Men

I have seen the whistling men
with a scribble and a wave and a hearty cheer
those factory boys at the sergeant's desk
with a kiss and a promise and a mug of beer
and the trains, and the trains, and the endless trains
with a song and a banner and a new frontier

I have seen the marching men
with a left and a right and a ragged wheel
those summer boys in an autumn world
with a fag and a sixpence and a dodgy deal
and the drills, and the drills, and the endless drills
with a fife and a fiddle and a drunken reel

I have seen the fighting men
with a mask and a pistol and a shrapnel flare
those stumbling boys in a sea of shit
with a bomb and a bucket and a muddy lair
and the noise, and the noise, and the endless noise
with a cry and a curse and a whispered prayer

I have seen the dying men
with an up and an over and a crazy scheme
those blasted boys in no man's land

with a shout and a volley and a final scream
and the blood, and the blood, and the endless blood
with a cross and a coffin and a crippled dream

And I have seen the weeping women
with a medal and a paper and a deep regret
those lonely girls at the farmyard gate
with a bottle and a baby and an unpaid debt
and the nights, and the nights, and the endless nights
when the sun goes down, we do not forget

Russell J Turner

Elaine Ewart

Heligoland is a small archipelago in the North Sea that has played a dramatic part in Europe's twentieth-century history of destruction. Once part of the British Empire, it was transferred into German hands in 1890, and subsequently fortified as a military base for the German navy. Heligoland's population, which had no choice in the fate of its beloved islands, was twice subjected to a forced evacuation to the German mainland. The islands suffered heavy bombardments towards the end of the Second World War, and afterwards, when the RAF used them for bombing practice. In 1947 the British military authorities blew up the islands entirely, and it was only after a lengthy campaign of peaceful protest that the Heligolanders were eventually allowed to return to their homeland and rebuild their town and communal life.

Elaine Ewart was the first Fenland Poet Laureate in 2012. Her work has been published in *Ink, Sweat and Tears*, *Dream Catcher, Friction* and *Ariadne's Thread*. She has published a short collection of poetry, *Fur, Feather and Fen* (2014). Elaine co-hosts Fen Speak, the monthly spoken word open mic night in Ely and Wisbech, and organises various other poetry events in fenland, as well as performing her poetry and giving talks throughout East Anglia and beyond.

Having recently finished a Master's degree in *Wild Writing: Literature and the Environment*, at the University of Essex, Elaine is planning a doctoral project on the cultural, literary and environmental significance of Heligoland, which was also the subject of her MA dissertation.

Elaine blogs at flightfeather.wordpress.com

Heligoland

Grün ist das Land,
rot ist die Kant,
weiß ist der Sand,
das sind die Farben von Helgoland.

(Heligoland motto)

red is the rock dust
blooming the sky,
stinging our eyes as we're carried away

over the sea

white is the bone,
blast-raised from rest;
a couple of old men are left to lay wreaths

in the wreckage

green are the leaves
of the mulberry tree,
sheltering space; we will kiss once again

under the blossom

Elaine Ewart

Nikki Marrone

'The inspiration for this piece was that growing up my father was a soldier in the army and so he travelled away a lot and I didn't really see him; and when he came back he was a different person.

So this poem was a way of trying to understand that on a personal level and exploring the potential consequences of war whilst realising that it wasn't really his fault that it happened.'

Solider

They say this is the price of bravery my dear
Your father's gone to war
To fight for me, to fight for you
For country and for pride
A hero forever more

But at six years old, I don't understand that
All I know is that he's gone
"I don't know what you're doing
Or even where you've gone
I just know your missing
And that I wish you'd come home soon."

At eight years old, I feel I understand
I feel my heart swell with pride
My father is a solider
He fights for *me*, he fights for *you*
For *country* and for *pride*
But as I start to watch the news, I start to think about it
The armour, the guns, the bombs, the fires
And the look in their eyes
At 8 years old I dream of death

And that you're never coming home.

But you do come home.
And at the age of eleven I see the damage they've done
You find peace in the dregs of a bottle
And follow the lines to feel whole
Fragments of your memories
A shattered soul
A cupboard for your guns
They broke you down, took away the bravery
Filled you up with sadness.

So I'm sick of being told peace is what he's fighting for
Pretending war doesn't pay for the rich and leave the poor
That all this blood, sweat, tears and toil
Isn't all for the price of oil
My father made me a solider
But I'll fight these wars with words
Won't carry arms or send off bombs
But tell it how it is
I will honour your brothers
But fight the men that sent you

Because I can’t imagine what you’ve seen
Or the things they made you do
But you, you are my father no more
Just a shadow of the man
A fleeting ghost
So full of hate
So full of rage
He picks up arms and points it proud
A stranger stares at me down the barrel of a gun

Nikki Marrone

Jacqueline Mulhallen

'I studied English at the University of New South Wales, and also French and so I discovered French poetry. I then studied in Finland, but, although travelling inspires me, I find academic study has the reverse effect. It seems to block my creativity, but working as an actor, as I did during this period, stimulates it. My lifelong love of Shelley's poetry has probably influenced me, but Sylvia Plath is another influence – I was in a play about her so I know lots of her poems by heart.

In 1987, *Lynx Theatre and Poetry* produced my play, *Sylvia* (about Sylvia Pankhurst, the suffragette and an antiwar campaigner in WW1) and in 1989, *Rebels and Friends* (about sisters Eva Gore-Booth, a pacifist, and Constance Markievicz, one of the leaders of the Easter Rising) in both of which I performed. These were very successful: *Sylvia* has been performed over 100 times and will be revived March 2015. In 2008 I was awarded a Ph.D. (Anglia Ruskin University). I have written *The Theatre of Shelley* (2010) and I am currently writing a biography of Shelley for Pluto Press. My poem *Debt* was commended in the 2014 Artemis Poetry Competition. (I) have had stories accepted by, among others, *BBC Radio 4* and *Spare Rib*.

I am deeply inspired to write by my anger at injustice, poverty and war. I have protested against war since the Vietnam demos in the

60s and have been an organiser of King's Lynn and Wisbech StoptheWar since 2003. In 1988, I was in Manchester performing *Sylvia*. That morning, my husband told me that CND were organising a competition for poems about the nuclear holocaust, so, before breakfast, I wrote *Persephone*. But because of the success of *Sylvia*, I became really busy – I completely forgot about the competition!'

Persephone

I don’t know what I’m doing in such a cold place.
I always loved the sun, and singing;
I danced with the others among the trees.

I was always the happiest of the girls,
Running across the green grass,
Gathering the blossoming twigs and crocuses, blue as the sea.
My laughter was my undoing.

If I had not laughed so happily he would never have noticed me:
‘I love your brightness,’ he said,
‘I wanted you to give gladness to this dim place.’
But I never laugh when I’m here.

I could have been still carefree by the seashore –
That land is so far distant now with its blossom;
I long for it six whole months of chilliness and silence,
Sometimes I wonder if I’ll ever go back again
Or if it’s all changed above ground.

And even when I’m walking in the sunshine,
Delighting in the ducklings and the lambs,
The chill of silence comes across my laughter;

One day no one will see the pussy willow;
All that will remain will be hard ashy dust,
Human bones where there were children,
Piles of rubble where there were cottages,
Shadows on Earth as well as in Hell.

Jacqueline Mulhallen

Philip Dunkerley

Philip Dunkerley has written poems for many years and now writes poems in retirement. He is active in poetry groups in the Peterborough, Stamford and Sleaford area, and Bourne where he now lives. A retired earth-scientist he published a collection of poems '*Sixty-Five*' in 2011 (available via Amazon) and has a strong interest in the Anglo-Saxon vernacular. He is a secularist and writes about the natural world and society from a humanist viewpoint.

'Between about 2007 and 2011 the Wiltshire town now known as Royal Wootton Bassett witnessed, with great dignity, over three hundred funeral processions pass along its high street. They were for British soldiers being repatriated through RAF Brize Norton from the wars in Iraq and Afghanistan. Many people feel that the Iraq war was started on a false premise, and that the war in Afghanistan was unjustifiable. British and American armed forces paid dearly for those wars and there were also many deaths among troops from other Nato countries. I wondered how family and friends coped when their loved ones were suddenly snatched away forever, and there were much larger death tolls of Iraqi and Afghan nationals, each loved by real people.

My own feelings are that the wars were not necessary and I felt sad at the institutionalised support provided, on all sides, by religious leaders for the conflicts. After watching, on television, yet another funeral cortege at Brize Norton, I wrote this poem as my protest against those who justify violence between societies.'

White Magic

A flag-draped box emerges from the plane,
Slowly; we see the drama played again.
Six strong men walking rigidly in time,
A story not repeating, but in rhyme
With what has, all too often, gone before:
Another coffin coming out the door
Of a huge plane. Six sad men hold upon
Reluctant shoulders, high, another one
Of their own number, breathing now no more.
Another brave young victim of the war.

Six servicemen, immaculately dressed,
An officer walks backwards, hand impressed
Against the coffin's head, to steady it
Descending from the ramp and ready it
For the arrival back on English soil
Of one more soldier, one who ever loyal
To orders of his officers has paid
The final price for failure of a raid.

The party reaches *terra firma*, then
Turning about, the Sergeant walks his men,
With slow and measured tread and all, dismayed,
Pay homage to the colleague who is laid

In peace within the casket that they bear.

A solitary figure standing there
Watches the slow procession pass him by,
Observes the slow parade with practiced eye,
Clutches the book that justifies the dead,
Hunches his shoulders, and then bows his head.

The slow procession nears the waiting hearse
The officer emits a quiet and terse
Command; in time at once the soldiers stop.
They take the burden that they bear atop
Their shoulders and in silent concert lower
The hard sad coffin to the polished floor
Of the long vehicle, long, shining, black.
The door comes down, the soldiers standing back.
The sable figure who has closed the door
Now makes a circle and walks on before
The creeping hearse, a top hat on his head,
Accoutrement of office for the dead.

The solitary figure with the book,
Brings up the rear, and in his hand the crook
That marks him as the shepherd of the sheep
That go to war, ostensibly to keep
Our country safe. For this the soldier died.
His cause was just; he had God on his side.

Philip Dunkerley

Pete Cardinal Cox

Pete has had various writings printed in the small-press for around thirty years, including the booklet Sack of Midnight (inspired by the medieval Welsh legends of The Mabinogion) published in 2010 by Hilltop Press of Huddersfield. As well as being the Peterborough Poet (2002 – 2003), he has also been Poet-in-Residence for Broadway Cemetery, Peterborough (2005 – 2008); winner of the John Clare Trust Poetry Prize (2009); and Poet-in-Residence of the church of St. John the Baptist, Peterborough (2012 – 2013) – which provided material for his act Lapsed Agnostic. He has also recently been performing an act based on the memoirs of my great-uncle who migrated to South Africa in 1875.

This poem dates back to the period I was Poet Laureate of Peterborough, late – 2002 through most of 2003. The inspiration came from the book Poppy Land by Clement Scott (published1886) about the area of Norfolk around Cromer, and from the painting Death the Bride by Thomas Cooper Gotch (painted around 1894/95). In the painting a pre-Raphaelite style woman in black veils stands amidst a field of red poppies. She struck me as an earlier incarnation of Neil Gaiman's Death from The Sandman comics. Thus these filtered through my thoughts of the First World War.

Poppy Land

After both Clement Scott and Thomas Cooper Gotch

Barbed wire divides the fields
Churned ready for the seed
And any weed that settles
Is fed when the youth bleed
Shelling keeps you awake too long
Thoughts turn to distant Poppy Land
Where stands a lonely tower
High above the broad sands

Cross the distant grey sea
Night's frozen desert sand
Beneath jungle storms of rain
Men lie in foreign land
She'll stand outside the cottage
As clouds colour in sunset
Crimson poppies in the field
And wonder why I'm not home yet

We'd wish a different harvest
Picking poppies from the corn

Sleep beneath a full moon
In the land where we's born
Don't wear them for the Generals
But for the lads in mud
The ones who gave their all
Paid in gore and blood

Pete Cox

Martin Figura

Martin's collection *Whistle (Arrowhead Press)* was shortlisted for the *Ted Hughes Award* and won the 2013 *Saboteur Award for Best Spoken Word Show.* He also won the 2010 Poetry Society Hamish Canham Prize. His pamphlets *Boring The Arse Off Young People* & *Arthur* are both published by *Nasty Little Press.* He works part-time at Norwich Writers' Centre.

'The poem is based on Upper Silesia and its turbulent history as a disputed territory. It is where Auschwitz Concentration Camp is and has changed hands a number of times. It was part of Germany before the Second World War, but is now part of Poland. The area is one of the most industrialised and polluted in Europe and where my father grew up. PG Wodehouse was interned there and is quoted as saying: "If this is Upper Silesia, what on earth must Lower Silesia be like?"

I visited in the early sixties and remember walking past the coal slag heaps and visited again two years ago.'

Coal

Caverns of fire growl deep underground
crack open the contaminated surface

so the murmur of voices can escape. The bones
of dukes and peasants, Bohemians, Prussians,

Mongol raiders and Moravians are pressed tight
into a fault line thin as a flag. The flag is the colour

of blood cells. Behind the buckling crosses
of window frames old men are dismantling clocks

on kitchen tables, looking for providence
amongst cogs and spiders.

And the black hills will join the sky and rain,
will pour down and bury this place.

Martin Figura

Samantha Weaver

'This poem is inspired by a hitchhiker we picked up on our way to Exmoor. Although we only shared a short car journey together he told us all about his life in the army and having to leave due to illness. He expressed a deep sense of loss and of being lost in terms of where to go next in life. The setting of a dark road up to the moor seemed like an uncanny context.'

Hitchhiker

Thumb out on the side of the road we pulled you in
late evening city speeding to the moor
and you from a War Crime Court hearing
telling us things we really didn't want to hear.
Running to the lay-by white eyed
"I live at the gateway to the moor, we'll pass right by my door."
It's crammed in the back
your breath on our necks
talking through the minefield of your life—
of time as a starving war rat, a camp orphan never leaving the
barracks, signed off with post traumatic syndrome,
chucked out by your landlord disturbed by your fist willingness.
Fast round a bend I think of the killing young, clinging to the thrill
of corners.
"She'll be surprised I'm home before her,
I can run fast but not that fast."
At last we pull in,
you pull yourself out
and we are left with a
firing line of unexpressed questions.

Samantha Weaver

J.S. Watts

J.S.Watts was born in London and now lives and writes in East Anglia. In between, she read English at Somerville College, Oxford and spent many years working in the UK education sector. Her poetry, short stories and book reviews appear in an eclectic range of publications in Britain, Canada, Australia and The States and have been broadcast on BBC and Independent Radio. In the past she has been Poetry Reviews Editor for Open Wide Magazine and Poetry Editor for Ethereal Tales. To date she has three books published and one in the pipeline: *Cats and Other Myths,* a poetry collection, is published by Lapwing Publications, as is a subsequent multi-award nominated poetry pamphlet, *Songs of Steelyard Sue*. Her first novel, *A Darker Moon,* a work of literary fiction and dark psychological fantasy, is published by Vagabondage Press. Her second novel, *Witchlight,* is due out from Vagabondage Press in Spring 2015. For further details please feel free to check out her website: www.jswatts.co.uk or her Facebook page at www.facebook.com/J.S.Watts.page.

'The poem *Broken Parts March Past* was sparked by my discomfort at the mind-set apparently prevalent in politicians and some areas of the armed forces, which puts so much emphasis on the pomp and circumstance of military display and regulation that reality and the human beings who are the serving men and women get overlooked. I object to the approach that glorifies war at the expense of the pity and horror of it; that revels in costly military ceremony, but does not adequately support those service personnel who are damaged by conflict; that demands the spit and polish of military display, but chooses to ignore the blood and guts reality, whilst sending out yet more young men and women to die or be maimed for their country. Regrettably, it's a mind-set that has been around for a long time.'

Broken Parts March Past

This, the song of broken parts,
may be hummed to the march tune
of your choice.
By a quick one, no two, brave boy;
don't let that leg stump
break your stride.

It is a theme for any time or season
but is tuned to the months
heavy with the fallen,
waiting for the drop
of russet and gold
to cover the fresh dug earth
with chestnut palls and
fig leaf yellow.

Take this eye patch, lass,
to keep the sand out of the socket.
I use two myself,
saves turning a blind eye.
Focus only on the major notes,
the gleam of self importance
in that polished sense of worth.
Respect the uniform,

not the chap who wears it.
There's no harm, my son,
in losing an arm
if your long, empty sleeve
is always worn with a tie,
top button clenched shut
to keep those thoughts in place.
You could see yourself in these shoes
if you had your eyes
or any feet left.
Hat squarely on your head when out of doors
until it's blown clean off, that is.

One family, one body,
one tune to step out to,
one, no two
and while I'd like to feel your loss
all empathy got cut off
in the drilling and the bashing
and the sharpened shiny tones
of the brass notes' clarion call.

Still, there's no shortage of raw parts
that'll polish up nice and fresh
before they're broken and ground
beneath the timeless drum roll
and the pride of the march.

J.S.Watts

Daisy Thurston - Gent

Daisy is a performance poet and playwright from Cambridge. She is a 2014 regional Hammer & Tongue Slam Finalist and has won competitions both in Cambridge and London. She has performed across London from venues such as the Royal Albert Hall, The Lost Theatre, The Genesis Cinema, The Gallery Café and The Poetry Café, and has even taken to the stage at the Bowery Poetry Club in New York.

Daisy has worked with musicians and dancers, as well as other spoken word artists, and is focused on the benefits of experimentation and artistic collaboration in live storytelling. Her poetry is often riddled with nostalgia; pulling expression and detail from moments that may have been previously overlooked.

The poem she has chosen for this collection takes inspiration from real conversations overheard during her time working in a pub.

Matchsticks

They form opinions over a Fosters Top,
Between roll ups.
Change their minds in the blink of an eye-
Half-locked on the waitress
Half-wasted.
They mention strategy
As if completely unaware
A terrifying lot of 'their'
Boys
Become no more than matchstick men
Sent home in boxes.

Try not to notice
They've barely been lit.

Another man sits quietly
The other side of me.
Fresh home from sanded landscapes where bombs are dropped more frequently
Than bass-drum beats in deep urban soundscapes.
His tank-like thighs strain across a beaten bar stool
He's staring into a Stella Artois.
His arms are covered in Koi carp
I ask him what they mean

He says, "one for every friend killed in Iraq"
All of them for peace.
Symbols that he
That we
Cannot forget.
Ink scars.

These midday lager men
To my right
Raise their voices.
Spit Tru Brit quips between sips.
Discuss 'tactics' now
Like football formations,
Except these mentioned men aren't toy soldiers
Made of plastic.
The referee won't send them to the bench
When it's all
Still to play for.

Daisy Thurston –Gent

Nigel Hilliam

'My grandfather served in the trenches on the Western Front in the Great War, suffering its conditions and horrors, but, like so many others, he would rarely share his experiences with us.

Ironically, for my A Level English, we studied the books and poems of the war but, other than verify certain aspects, he would not be drawn into describing many incidents or his feelings at the time or since.

I have no doubt that he saw active combat, death, horrific injuries, the effects of gas, the torment of suffering horses & exposure to the elements of cold & wet. He would also have seen at first hand the transformation of young, patriotic boys into weary, battle-hardened men who endured the waste, despair & pity of war. I am sure that he thrived on the camaraderie of his peers but also ached for the comforts of family & home.

It was this lack of knowledge that led me to study & imagine the life of soldiers in the war & also those left at home. Ultimately this became the inspiration that persuaded me to try to express my thoughts in poetry – it was, at times, as if he was guiding my hand as I wrote.

Times may change & wars still rage across the world, but the First World War was unique in its scale, devastation & disregard for human life. Whilst we may not have learnt from its lessons, we can only hope that its like will never be seen again.

It is not my place to judge the rights or wrongs of war but I feel a duty to express the effects that it must have had on the most important thing in life – people.'

The Angel of Mercy

Ghostly shards of moonlight cut through the mist
And pierced the abyss of the shell-hole like
Searchlights.
Alone, I curled into my mother–earth,
Praying for an angel of mercy to bring the peace of sleep.

But when he came he was not the angel.
High up on the ledge I saw his greycoat, his rifle – the reaper's
Scythe.
Instinct kicked, safety clicked and my gun raised to
Meet his aim.
Time stood still to watch the kill.

In that stare we saw our souls.
The call to arms, the boyish haste, the bitter truth, the
Utter waste.
Dimly echoed a haunting voice, 'kill or be killed', the
Only choice.
But my finger lingered to delay the end.

Then his shoulders sagged, his breath like smoke.
Even the devil can gorge ‘til sick.
Into the haze he floated away.
Dead or alive, into oblivion.

Nigel Hilliam

Jonathan Totman

Jonathan was born in Sussex and studied psychology and philosophy at Oxford University. He went on to train as a clinical psychologist in London before moving to Ely in 2013, where he lives with his partner and cat.

Jonathan is a member of the London-based group *Highgate Poets* and co-edited their 2014 anthology, *The Space it Might Take*. His poems have been published or are forthcoming in various magazines including *Orbis, Obsessed with Pipework*, *The Cannon's Mouth* and *The Dawntreader*. He was recently shortlisted in the *Holland Park Press* competition and won third place in the 2014 Fenland Poet Laureate awards.

The Veteran was inspired in part by Jonathan's work as a clinical psychologist. It is a poem about the trauma of war and its lasting impact both on those who witness it first hand and their loved ones. But it is also about the repercussive effects of *any* conflict (personal, interpersonal, political…) and how we can connect when a relationship has become fractured; how we can survive when a wound refuses to heal.

<u>The Veteran</u>

She is diplomat here, in the war-torn city
of his mind. Barred from the upper echelons,

she snatches words with representative
after representative – that quiet man

who knew him from before; the drinker,
who'd rather argue than be touched;

and that man who looks right through her
and hates the smell of burning meat.

*

They walk together still, old familiar routes.
She sees him calculating advantages

on the golf-course, thinking this would be
a piss-poor position for a counter-attack.

The key to surviving an ambush,
he told her once, *is to override instinct*

and head towards your attackers -
retreat, and you'll run straight into their arms.

*

Lately, she's noticed, he's taken to watching bees –
some solace, perhaps, in their ceaseless drone.

Did you know, she asks him at breakfast,
that to produce a jar of honey, a bee has to travel

the equivalent of three times around the world?
Later, she sees a fleet of tiny Chinooks circling

the honeysuckle; a man in thick cottons
and helmet patrolling the garden.

*

He carries around a stick of Vicks VapoRub,
sniffs it on the tube to convince himself

he's here and it's now. She's on board,
checks he's remembered and doesn't ask why

she has less influence than a whiff of strong scent.
He keeps it in his pocket with a post-it note:

You're safe, you're strong, this feeling will pass.
You're a good person going through a difficult time.

*

On the train home, his head lolls in half-sleep,
sinking to her shoulder then jerking up.

She sees him waking, groggy, *like death,*
laughing off the night's drinking

and not remembering how he kissed
her on the platform while she fumbled

for her ticket. She will laugh too, she supposes,
bring him coffee, pills for his acceptable pain.

Jonathan Totman

Rachel Rose Reid

Raised in the UK on folk music, migrant heritage & urban jungle, Rachel Rose Reid combines all three to build bridges between oral tradition & contemporary spoken word.

She has written and performed for Billy Bragg, BBC Radio 3, Southbank Centre, Royal Shakespeare Company, Barbican, London Symphony Orchestra, as well as creating material in partnership with music acts from hip hop bands to a cappella choirs.

Rachel has been a Resident Artist at the EFDSS, exploring the tales carried to England by recent migrants and her own ancestors. She was Writer in Residence for the Dickens Bicentenary, and her immersive tale can still be found on the handheld audio guides at the Charles Dickens Museum.

Her show *I'm Hans Christian Andersen* has received high praise in international press, and she regularly performs with musician Robin Grey in *Three Acres & A Cow: A History of Land Rights and People's Protest in Folk Song & Story.*

"Immense skill and breathless conviction. There's no faulting Reid's command of her craft" The Times

You can find out more about her work at **www.rachelrosereid.com**

'In the height of World War One centennial ceremonies and memorial events, the news of the air raids on Islamic State strongholds seemed to slip in without any kind of announcement.

It seemed clear to me that all lives lost in this ongoing War on Terror (regardless of the 'side' taken), will not have such a way to be remembered or honoured. There's no clear end. So there cannot be distance, reflection, mourning or moving on, something which seems essential for growth and change.'

On Waking Up

"Our war on terror begins with al Qaeda, but it does not end there. It will not end until every terrorist group of global reach has been found, stopped and defeated." George W Bush, 20 September 2011

"Rig the roads with explosives for them. Attack their bases. Raid their homes. Cut off their heads. Do not let them feel secure. Hunt them wherever they may be. Turn their worldly life into fear and fire. Remove their families from their homes and thereafter blow up their homes." Abu Muhammad al---Adnani, ISIS, 22 September 2014 [I could go on...]

There will be no Memorial Day for this.
No one will read a soldier's poem, see
Wild roses growing in the rubble
Jasmine scrambling up the wall
And pick them as the symbol for lost youth.

There will be no Morning when we suit---up
Sat in haunted contemplation
Wreathed in fading eulogies
Clocks will not stop.
This One is a task that does not end.

There will be no Archive, carefully compiled

Letters to unknown soldiers,
Sons and daughters,
Righteous, heathen, forced, foolish,
Or just walking the wrong way home.

There will be no great---grandma
Cosily recalling the relief, how,

The day when It was over
Streets were thickly packed with song;
Wide---eyed school kids, scribbling down her memoir for posterity.

No Leader will commission the creation of
Requiem, Qasida, Psalm,
Stone Memorial, Lights Out night,
Peace Garden, Remembrance Meeting Hall,
Crimson blossoms bleeding from our monuments, Two Minutes'
Silence.

There will be no moment for regret, for
Soft hearts, listening, confusion,
No room for error, refuge, thought,

No time to question, comment, lose.
There will be no End; we have been told.

There will be no pillow soft enough to sleep on.
Lost feathers on the wind
Impossible to gather in

Rachel Rose Reid

Gram Joel Davies

Gram Joel Davies feels connected to all wetland landscapes, and a lot of his poetry carries their watermark. His work has appeared over the years in journals online and in print, including *The Centrifugal Eye*, *The Lake* and *The Journal*. His archived writings can be read at *Poplar Verse*(www.poplarverse.wordpress.com) and he uses Twitter as @poplarist.

The white poplar, *populus alba*, is his favourite tree. Perhaps because it chooses to exist on the boundaries between water and soil. Or because the silver shake of its leaves is an amalgam of liquid and solid.

'It is difficult to introduce poetry, because a poem is never *about* something. Like every human life, a poem is a thing whose meaning is its whole self. *I Revisit the Pillbox* tries to think about war as cultural memory. A child, whose impulse is to protect life, plays in the ruins of old fortifications. We grow, become, leave our mark. It is often hard to visualise war truly, but when we forget the details of individual life, that is the tragedy, which poetry might assuage. Every memorial states "This is who I am. I was here." It is something that needs to be revisited, continuously.'

I Revisit the Pillbox

where we ran from fields, to a concrete cubicle
adventure. A slab-nest base of ack-ack
and ratter-tatter. On its grenade-
stopping pillar, charcoal genitals, drawn
after someone's lager-can cracking fool vigil.

Below, the bridge-edge falls into big-E teeth
of missing masonry. I watch the same centuries
in stone become tumbledown, still hanging.

Listen how it trembles, the stream telling
ears what feet think. Where pipeline warrens

are diagrammatic of burst sycamore roots,
of worm-casts and aorta. Remember:

we found a noose of orange wire, ripped
it in horror, ran the knot to nothing, flung it
in the water. Grass still has evening's odour, over
which daddy-long-legs scatter, their slapstick
made acrobatic in long blades. We noticed
how it must feel to fit -- not be the jester

on the precipice. Fallen memory, a sucking

taste, biting sloe berry. Dead concrete boxes
can thrill us. A broken edge hold us.

The brook loops through the rocks

which did plummet, and I scribe initials
with a brick-pattern ember (its touch
like polyester) on the wall of this burrow
block: sigils for ancient decades later.

Gram Joel Davies

Anthony Smith

'As a young idealist I always shunned Remembrance Day in the belief that it somehow attempts to justify war. The acres of unmarked graves sickened me, and the anonymous red poppy seemed to further turn these real human tragedies into nothing more than a symbol. But as I have grown older I have come to understand that our philosophies and principles are worthless unless they speak for, care for, the human self. It may be that the pomp and ceremony of Remembrance Day stands as a political act, just as war itself does – but it remains a fact that war is waged at the cost of human lives on the battlefield and on the home front. So I wanted to create a piece that would simultaneously decry the state's imposition of jingoist symbolism upon our most horrific history, whilst yet saluting the fallen.

I have been writing and performing poetry for over twenty years. All of my work attempts to speak to the individual – shunning 'issues' and 'politics' as I believe people are at their very best when they are on their own; and at their very worst when acting (or speaking) in groups. I also believe that all of us have the ability to think critically, that we do not in fact need to be taught, or preached to. So I offer my poem here not as a manifesto, or absolute truth – but rather as one possible perspective. I do hope you can share this view, but if not, that you can resist the taking up of arms!

Those who do enjoy this piece may welcome the news that I have a full pamphlet collection just released in collaboration with the mental health charity ‘Second Chance’, entitled “Joy, Fear and Fuck It”.’

The 11th Minute of the 11th hour

Don't remember me with silence
As though you regret I gave my life
Don't shuffle in embarrassment
And count the seconds ticking by
Don't think of us as numbers
You were prepared to pay this price
Don't remember me with silence
Celebrate you are alive

Don't remember me with symbols
As though they could signify
Don't forget the individuals
You set up on your bloody lines
Don't imagine there's a difference
In today's accountants eyes
Don't remember me with symbols
I'm more than the question 'Why'

The beast cannot be counted
Such numbers will tell lies
Life is not an algebra
Unmarked graves are not a sign
Don't remember me with silence
Don't conscript me to that good night

Don't remember me with silence

Celebrate you are alive

Ant Smith

Josh Bone

'..all we have: the necessities of each day, the passion.' Adelida prado

Born in 1990 Josh grew up in Ely, studied art, design and illustration for six years then, after graduating from Falmouth university in 2011, turned back to confront some niggling hang ups; words, writing, and dyslexia.

Having finished a cert TEFL course in 2012, he spent a year in Tokyo teaching English and started to play with words to make images.

Now a full time artist, the habit of letting words stop whatever he happens to be doing has stuck and he is working on a pamphlet of work alongside visual art projects.

Home from War

Chrome lips, bite down on soil
nail clippers in my right hand
in the sink radio gongs
black hair they meet and go

the same way gongs like before

my plough bit has sharpened
I dig a different way now
my back is alert
and this is unnerving I guess

our differences have exploded

my brain is what holds this,
bed as a Bed and not that table laid and,
arms as Arms, they are waiting,

legs as Legs.

white and red, the barbers

I push the dirt and bits of nail

like tea leaves with a silver spoon

turning my face, concave, and milk

and sugar, convex, lift the bag

grip

can flicker - one

with street lights

turning day over - two

the table -three

lift the bag-

with the others-

it's not a fun fair-

strong man-

roll upweights like that-

numbers in jars-

roll up

k, no problem, I cooked so see you in thirty

my eyes hold up mirrors

but they cannot hold that steam

my ears hold up apologies

that don't fit us

we know different things that ring

Josh Bone

Mike Bannister

'A singular moment in the life of a child in time of war. My parents, regardless of the fear, the violence and the hurt, demonstrate their essential conviction that Humanity, above all else, must prevail in the end.

The poem attempts to make memorable this far reaching philosophy, in a way that is truthful to the occasion, capturing both the love and the pathos, the universal bonds that render Peace possible.'

After the Peace

For Marcella

Prisoners of war, counting off the days,
came in for Sunday tea; white damask,
dainty salad, an egg perhaps, thin bread,
a simple cake, our mother's plain defiance
of enduring want; her way of showing
what trouble she was still prepared to take.

Hans, Max and Josef, out of Solingen, reported
prompt at four and stayed 'til nine, in clean
fatigues and shiny boots, their faces weathered
red as the earth they furrowed for their keep.

First it was names, shy smiles, and downward
glances, then pidgin-talk about the state of things,
how like a snail time was, the waste of war, the longing
and the doubt. Even at three foot five, I knew for sure,
what was happening here was preferable.

Beside the fire, we shared familial tales
of flight, migration, and our German kin;
while father tuned his ancient table-harp,
and in the sweetest tenor, gave us first

Robin Adair, the melancholy *Turtle Dove*
and last, as if to grace that gathering
with all he had to give, began
to his own slow chords, *The Lorelei* .

It was the first and last time ever I saw
a man, four men, faces wet with tears,
re-capture what was left of harmony;
their song, some kind of forgotten road
we followed, miles away from war.

Mike Bannister

<u>Robin Shorey</u>

Robin Shorey was born in Johannesburg in 1949, graduating in Psychology from the University of Queensland, Brisbane in 1980. The poem *Family History* grew out of his personal experiences of how the emotional and spiritual traumas of war are transferred from generation to generation.

Family History

One moon mad evening
as bullets tore the night apart
and shells out-shrieked his shriek
he cried out with fear and dived into
a foxhole yelling
forgive me forgive me
as though it were him that had made the night scream
not them.

One moon mad evening
as I slept my snuffled sleep
harsh screams ripped at the fabric of my warmth
casting my soft flesh into frozen steel.
Terrified I fell into a black hole screaming
forgive me forgive me
as though it were I who tore the night apart
not them.

I am older now and cough wetly in the night
and still cry out at the dark sky
forgive me forgive me

as though it were that which clenched my heart to grief

not I.

Robin Shorey

Acknowledgements

I have many people to thank for their support in the making of this book. Firstly, Alan Gaughran for his endless hours of artistic brilliance. To Professor Benjamin Zephaniah for his inspirational work and invaluable assistance. To James Rippin and Keith Rippin for unfathomable technical aid. To my best friend in the world Richard McNally for all his encouragement and advice. To Leanne Moden, Elaine Ewart, William Alderson and Jackie Malhullen for entertaining my eccentricities and aid in all things poetic. To my parents, all three, for remaining proud and supportive despite my insistence on a poverty stricken poetry career. And last but not least, all the wonderfully talented poets in the anthology who have blown me away with their insight and ability.